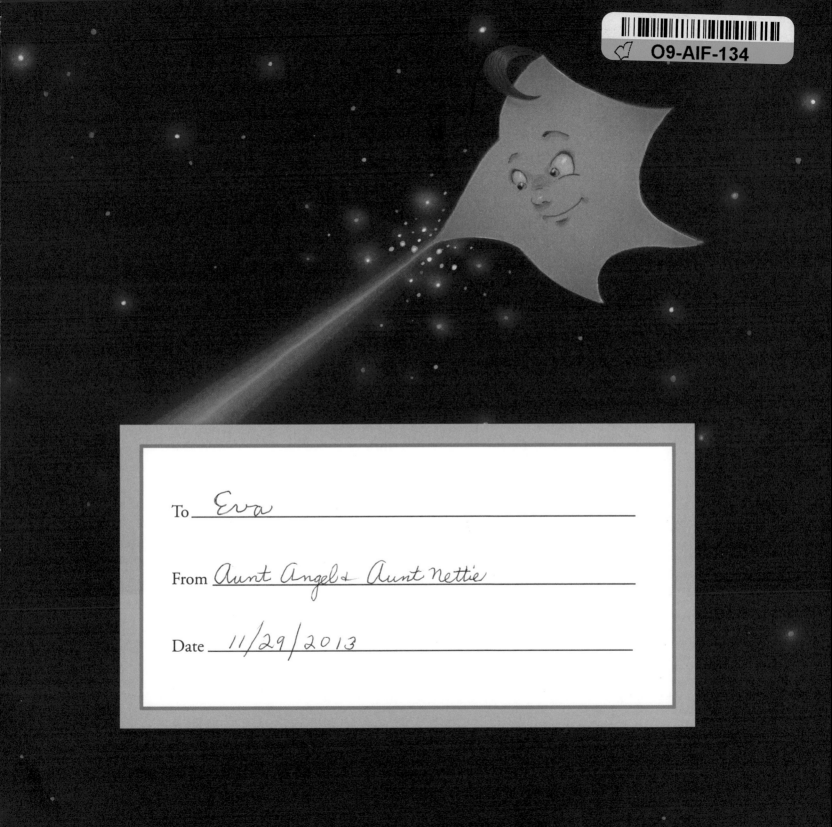

To _Eva_

From _Aunt Angel & Aunt Nettie_

Date _11/29/2013_

Little
Star

Anthony DeStefano
illustrated by Mark Elliott

HARVEST HOUSE PUBLISHERS
EUGENE, OREGON

Little Star

Text copyright © 2010 by Anthony DeStefano
Illustrations copyright © 2010 by Mark Elliott

Published by Harvest House Publishers in 2013
Eugene, Oregon 97402
www.harvesthousepublishers.com

ISBN 978-0-7369-5859-2

Design and production by Katie Brady Design, Eugene, Oregon

All Scripture verses are taken from the New King James Version. Copyright © 1982 by Thomas Nelson, Inc. Used by permission.
All rights reserved.

Previously published by Waterbrook Press, Colorado Springs, Colorado, in 2010

The Mom's Choice Awards Honoring Excellence logo is a trademark of the Mom's Choice Awards. For more information:

Mom's Choice Awards
787.410.9409
help@momschoiceawards.com

Printed in China

13 14 15 16 17 18 19 20 / LP / 10 9 8 7 6 5 4 3 2 1

This book is for my nephews,
Salvatore, Andrew, and Matthew,
and my niece, Diana.
—ANTHONY DESTEFANO

This book is for Emma and
for Grace, two little stars.
—MARK ELLIOTT

...and behold, the star which they had seen in the East went before them, till it came and stood over where the young Child was.

MATTHEW 2:9

For God so loved the world that He gave His only begotten Son, that whoever believes in Him should not perish but have everlasting life.

JOHN 3:16

"Dad, which one is the Christmas star?"
the boy asked, straining his eyes as he
looked out at the clear, dark sky.

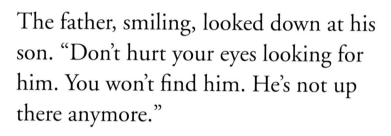

The father, smiling, looked down at his son. "Don't hurt your eyes looking for him. You won't find him. He's not up there anymore."

"Where is he? Where did he go?"

"You mean I never told you the story of the Christmas star before?"

"No, Dad, never." The boy shook his head. "Please tell me."

Well, a long time ago, in the farthest corner of the universe, there was a tiny star. In fact, he was the smallest star in the heavens. His name was Little Star.

Little Star was sad and lonely. The other stars didn't make fun of him. They simply ignored him because he was so tiny. But what can be worse for a star than to be ignored? After all, stars do little more than decorate the sky. They help pass the long evenings by "twinkle-talk."

And there was a lot of twinkling going on. The other stars were all talking about a rumor they had heard for ages—a rumor that a king would soon be born on a faraway planet called Earth.

It was known that the king had a special message
that would change the whole world forever.

As the great day approached,
excitement among the stars began
to build. A special reward was to be
given to the star who could shine the
brightest on the night the baby king
was born.

LITTLE STAR

In preparation, the stars were being cleaned and dusted by long-tailed comets. This made them twinkle and sparkle and give off a much stronger light.

All except Little Star who was being ignored again, despite his tears.

Little Star was so sad that his points drooped.
How could an undusted star have any chance
of winning the reward?

Finally, on the coldest night of the year, one of the stars yelled, "It's happening! It's happening! The king is going to be born!"

Far below, in the small village of Bethlehem, Little Star could see two people: a woman sitting on a donkey and a man walking beside her.

He watched as they searched for somewhere to rest. It was bitter cold, and Little Star felt sorry for them. Wherever they went no one seemed to want them.

People can be cruel too, he thought.

At last, the man and woman located a place to stay. It was a shabby stable, but at least it gave them protection against the icy winds.

This is a strange way for a king to be born, thought Little Star.

Then, with only the silent stars as witnesses, the child was born. The mother wrapped the baby in a blanket and carefully placed him in a straw-filled manger. The baby's name was Jesus.

"He can't be a king," one of the stars said.
"Kings aren't born poor. We've been fooled." Feeling
disappointed, many of the other stars agreed. But
Little Star kept looking down at the baby. Suddenly a thought
came to him.

"I think I understand," Little Star cried out.
"The baby Jesus IS a king!

He's just little!"

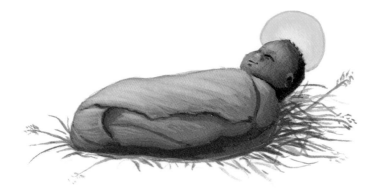

Little Star knew that Jesus could have chosen to be born in a palace, surrounded by riches, but instead, he had humbled himself to be born in a stable. He didn't want to be rich and important. He wanted to be like the poorest of the poor. Jesus wanted to be born little to show all the people of the world that he loved them, no matter how small or poor they were.

Of all the stars in the heavens, Little Star was the only one to understand the king's message.

His message was *love*.

Little Star's heart was bursting with joy. He wanted so badly to touch the child. Trying as hard as he could, he used all his strength and might to reach out with his light toward the earth.

Burning brighter and brighter, he extended
his rays down to the village of Bethlehem,
into the cold stable, warming and lighting
it with his love.

The other stars were amazed. They had never seen Little Star so big and bright. But they were scared that he was burning too brightly for such a small star. "Stop!" they all yelled. "Stop or you'll burn yourself out!"

Little Star could not hear their warnings. He was only aware of the child in the cold stable. All through the long, cold night, Little Star burned as brightly as he could so the baby Jesus could be warm.

When dawn came, the star that no one
had ever noticed was tiny and gray.
"Little Star is gone," the other stars cried.
"He burned himself out."

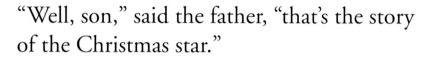

"Well, son," said the father, "that's the story of the Christmas star."

"But he's gone." The boy felt very sad.

"No, he's not. He's not gone at all."

The father patted his son's hand to reassure him. "You see, Little Star did a wonderful thing that night in Bethlehem. He gave his life so the baby Jesus could be warm. And God gave him a great reward in return. Little Star will be remembered forever and ever."

"You mean Little Star isn't gone?" the boy asked.

"No, he's alive!" the father said. "Every Christmas, when we celebrate Jesus' birthday, people all over the world place a star on top of their Christmas tree to remember him."

The boy looked up at the star on top of the Christmas tree and smiled.

The End